Empath:

Highly Sensitive Person's Handbook for Mastering Your Gift, Setting Your Boundaries & Thriving in a Chaotic World

ROZELLA HART

BONUS: BOOK CLUB INVITE

Before we get started with this Empath book, we wanted to tell you how much we appreciate you as a reader, and that we want to invite you to our Free Book Club.

When you subscribe, you get first access to discounted and free new releases from or small publishing house, Walnut Publishing.

Claim your invite at www.walnutpub.com.

Thanks for buying, and enjoy reading.

Note from the Author

Thank you for purchasing "Empath: Highly Sensitive Person's Handbook for Mastering Your Gift, Setting Your Boundaries & Thriving in a Chaotic World."

I hope you will learn a lot of valuable information that you can apply to your own life, as well as have some fun and be entertained!

I worked hard to write this book with you, my reader, in mind. Whether you enjoyed the book, or you think I got some things wrong, I'd love to hear from you.

I personally read all my reviews on Amazon, and love to hear from my readers. If you can take a minute to just write at least one line about what you thought of my book, I'd be really grateful.

Type this URL into your browser to go straight to the review page for this book: bit.ly/empathreview

I really appreciate it, and now, let's get to the book!

—Rozella Hart

TABLE OF CONTENTS

1 INTRODUCTION

HELLO!

THANK YOU FOR CHOOSING to read this book about the empathic gift. I am sure it will be of great use to you, no matter what stage you are at in your journey as an empath.

Maybe you are just learning what an empath is and think you might be one. Maybe you've heard this word "empath" in a negative context before, but don't worry; to be an empath is to be gifted in a way most people are not, and simply learning about your gift will help you find greater happiness than you imagined possible.

Maybe you are struggling with feeling overwhelmed by your friendships and the negative energy surrounding you day in and day out. This book will help you control your empathic gift and use it to thrive rather than to be drained by it.

Maybe you are deep into the empathic journey and you find yourself borrowing energy from somewhere outside yourself day after day, only to have to return that energy at the end of the day. You are defined by negative energy and are struggling with addictions and relationship troubles at every turn, and you do not know where to turn. This book is for you, too.

Whether you are wondering whether you are an empath or you are reading to learn to manage and thrive with your empathic gift, this book will be a great help and encouragement to you. We will cover everything from building positive relationships, to addiction and recovery, to ending toxic relationships and many things in between.

Are you ready to change your life for the better? Are you ready to find the happiness you have been seeking as an empath? Then buckle up, settle in, and let's get started.

2 AM I AN EMPATH?

THE FIRST STEP IN YOUR Empath journey is to correctly identify yourself as one.

How do you know if you are an empath? What are the character traits of an empath? How does an empath act in relationships? These are excellent questions to which you must know the answers if you are to thrive as an empath. I have developed five categories of characteristics that empaths often exhibit to help you identify whether you are an empath.

The five categories of empathic characteristics are as follows: character traits that empaths exhibit, how empaths act in relationships, empathic lifestyle, how others respond to empaths, and the struggles that empaths face because of their emotionally sensitive nature toward others' feelings. If you identify with one of more of these categories, it is likely you have some empathic abilities, but in the next chapter, we will provide a helpful quiz so that you can know once and for all if you have the rare gift of an empath.

Character Traits

The empath often exhibits some character traits that are connected to his or her empathic abilities. These character traits are not only found in the empathic portion of the population, but they are more distinct and pronounced among empaths.

First, the empath is highly sensitive. This does not mean the empath is emotionally weak or anything of the sort. Rather, it means that your senses are tuned into others' feelings in a stronger way than the average person. Empaths can determine what another person is feeling simply by looking at or talking with them.

Empaths are also very intuitive because of this sensitivity. They can distinguish emotions in others based on very little input. Therefore, they seem to have an uncanny sense of what other people are feeling. Sometimes, they also seem to know what it going to happen before it occurs. For example, you might be able to predict the outcome of a conversation with great precision. This intuition in empaths sometimes draws them into the metaphysical realm to become psychics and soothsayers. Even if they decide not to enter the spiritual realm in that way, empaths find they can use their intuition to their advantage, something we will look at later in this book.

Besides being sensitive and intuitive, empaths often have highly-tuned senses. If you can hear or see better than most other people; you might be an empath. Empaths are constantly searching for information about the world around them, whether it be visual, auditory, emotional, or spiritual. This allows the empath to pick up on cues and occurrences that other people usually miss, such as hearing conversations from across the room or hearing a door open when the noise level in the room is crowded with people's conversations and laughter.

The way that empaths constantly seek information about the world around them leads us to the next character trait of empaths: an inquisitive mind. The empath asks questions about why things are the way they are, and looks to answer those questions. As a result, the empath usually has a deeper understanding of his or her world than the average person.

The last character traits exhibited by many empaths are creativity and imagination. The empath is often highly imaginative and artistic. He or she participates in some type of writing or art, if it is possible, because he or she is compelled to create and express what is bottled up inside.

Empaths In Relationships

There are a few things that define empaths' relationships.

First, empaths often enter too quickly into relationships and may become overwhelmed by the intimacy. The relationships in this context are not necessarily romantic relationships. Many times, even in a friendship, you will share too much of your personal life or feelings and then become overwhelmed by the closeness that the sharing creates. Empaths desire emotional depth so much that they often subconsciously try to force it by sharing too much of themselves at once. This results in a post-sharing awkwardness as the empath realizes he or she is not comfortable enough to have shared what was shared.

Another characteristic of empathic relationships is that empaths have big hearts and often overextend themselves in giving. This might be in a single relationship or result from the fact that the you are pouring your whole self into multiple friendships. Either way, empaths usually find themselves depleted of emotional energy because of how much is given away in friendships and relationships.

Empaths also blame themselves for any time they are mistreated in a relationship. This leads to abusive and codependent relationships. Any time you are treated badly or wrongly, you will make an excuse for the other person's behavior because you understand the other person's motives. You will then take on responsibility for the behavior because you anticipated that the other person would respond in that way to the situation. Empaths feel like they should have prevented the situation from arising in the first place.

Empathic Lifestyle

Often, empaths are introverted. This occurs because being around other people depletes the empath's pool of emotional energy. You will need to take time to yourself if you are an empath, not necessarily because you do not enjoy being with others, but because you need to restore some of the energy that you lose during your interactions with other people.

As an empath, you can restore emotional energy by spending time in nature. Just being alone in your house will not restore your energy to the same level as taking a stroll in the woods or park would. Your spiritual and emotional self finds that nature is replenishing and refreshing, whereas being around people is often draining. This subconscious appreciation of nature is more pronounced in empaths because of their deep connection to the natural world and the elements.

Another trait to look for in empaths is a need for stimulation on a deeper level than surface activities. Empaths often become bored and tune out if their minds are not engaged. As an empath, you might have found that, in school, you were constantly getting in trouble for daydreaming or not paying attention when your classwork was too easy. This means that you were looking for something more engaging mentally and emotionally to draw your attention. This is not a defect, but part of your gift.

Often, empaths like to live in simple and clutter-free living spaces due to their high sensitivity to environment. Empaths' minds are already so cluttered by all the emotions and feelings of those around them that they often do not feel equipped to deal with an elaborate living space. Instead, you might prefer a minimalistic space, with just a few decorations and little mess.

As cliché as it may sound, empaths often embody the definition of a "free spirit." As an empath, you might find yourself feeling trapped by rules, schedules, and routines. Your regular schedule might sometimes feel like a cage from which you just want to break free. You desire spontaneity and look for ways to break the rules, even in small ways, like walking on the grass instead of on the pavement.

Finally, as an empath, you might discover that you are drawn to metaphysical and holistic therapies. You might have been diagnosed with a mental health disorder, but medications and typical therapies are not healing you as well as you would like. You seek spiritual answers and answers in the metaphysical realm. You seek spiritual practices like yoga, prayer, and meditation to help relieve your symptoms. Indeed, you will find that these practices help even more than the therapy and medication regimen. You are not alone in this. Your empathic brothers and sisters can relate.

Interactions With Empaths

There are a couple of ways that people generally react to empaths.

One of the ways is to target them for unloading. Empaths are often the victims of parasitic individuals who want only to shift their own burden onto someone else, and the empath is an easy target because he or she wants to help ease everyone's pain. You might find that you are the one that everyone calls when a life crisis occurs. Your friend calls you about every breakup and vents, your boyfriend or girlfriend unloads all the stresses from work onto you, your mother tells you all about her problems with your father, and none of them seem concerned for your well-being. As an empath, you are the target for everyone's venting and are asked to take on others' burdens more often than anyone else.

Another response to empaths, especially upon first meeting them, is to assume they are shy and moody. People who are empaths can sometimes come off as disconnected or aloof, but this is simply because, as you might know, you are protecting yourself from feeling the emotions of everyone in the room so that you are not overwhelmed. You are not trying to be rude, but you are hoping to reserve your energy for the interactions that need it.

Struggles Facing Empaths

The struggles facing the empath are numerous, and we will take a deeper look at them in a future chapter. For now, to help you identify whether you are an empath, we will outline a few of the more common difficulties with which empaths wrestle.

First, empaths struggle with distinguishing their emotions from the emotions of those around them. This can lead to other problems, such as empaths agreeing to something that they do not themselves want to do because they are feeling the emotions of other people rather than feeling their own. This issue of distinguishing emotions leads to a lot of confusion and frustration so that you might find yourself very irritable around other people. You must be especially careful that you do not let yourself be taken advantage of, as failing to distinguish between emotions leaves you open to abusive behaviors like sexual coercion.

Empaths also find it hard to relax and feel at ease in a group. There are so many emotions floating around and so many perspectives represented in a group that an empath, who feels them all, becomes easily overwhelmed. Crowded places can be very difficult for you as an empath.

As an empath, you find it hard to be present with a judgmental person. Judgmental people reek of negative energy, and you will find it incredibly difficult to abide the comments, thoughts, and feelings of a judgmental person. You might have the courage to stand up to this person for the victim of their judgmental ways, but this too will deplete your emotional energy, so it sometimes is best to just avoid judgmental people altogether.

An empath often struggles with fatigue. You are using so much energy to feel and cope with the emotions of those around you that you have little, if any, left to deal with your own inner world. This type of fatigue does not go away with any amount of sleep. Instead, the energy must be replenished through immersing yourself in nature or spending time around kind people full of positive energy.

Addictions are another struggle for an empath. Coping with more than just their own emotions, empaths often turn to binge-eating, anorexia, drug addiction, or self-harm as a means of expressing and dealing with the emotions that are plaguing them.

3 100-Point Empath Quiz

Putting It All Together: Are You An Empath?

In this chapter, we have provided a quiz to help you determine whether or not you are an empath. It should take less than 10-15 minutes to complete.

To tell whether you are an empath or not, mark a 0 (never true) to a 5 (true all the time) next to the following statements:

1)   Are you highly sensitive to the emotions, thoughts, or feelings of those around you? ___
2)   Are you often able to predict the outcome of something, especially in social situations? ___
3)   Is your sense of hearing highly developed and/or can you hear things that other people do not catch? ___

4) Do you often ask why things are the way they are or seek to understand how things work? ___

5) Are you artistic or do you appreciate art and writing? ___

6) Do you get into relationships quickly or become overwhelmed by the quick pace of your relationships? ___

7) Do you feel drained of energy because you are always giving? ___

8) Is your first thought "What did I do wrong?" when you are mistreated by someone? ___

9) Do you find yourself feeling replenished in nature? ___

10) Do activities that feel mindless or aren't challenging make you space out? ___

11) Do you prefer to keep your living space free of clutter? ___

12) Do you feel trapped by rules or routines? ___

13) Do you seek spiritual answers to your problems? ___

14) Do you find that unloaders and parasitic individuals gravitate toward you? ___

15) Are you seen as introverted, shy, aloof, moody, or disconnected?

___

16) Do you struggle to sort out which emotions belong to you and which belong to those around you? ___

17) Is it difficult and sometimes overwhelming to be part of a crowd?

___

18) Do you find it draining to be with people who are judgmental? ___

19) Are you constantly tired and unable to get relief no matter how much you sleep? ___

20) Do you have any addictive behaviors (eating disorders, substance abuse, self-harm, etc.)? ___

Now, add up your scores for each question. You should come up with a number between 0 and 100.

.

0-9: You are likely not an empath. This does not mean you cannot be kind or compassionate, only that you might have to work a little harder to understand another person's point of view. You might not have the empathic gift, but you are blessed with the desire to understand those around you, and you would be a great friend or partner for anyone. The rest of this book still applies to you, as you seek to give of yourself to those around you and must be careful in doing so.

10-29: You have a bit of the empathic gift. Although it is weaker than in most empaths, you can develop it in order to become stronger and to help you thrive. You have the potential to understand others on a deeper level than the average person, but you must also be wary of the struggles facing the empath.

30-59: You are almost definitely an empath. Your gift is somewhat strong, but it could be developed more. You likely have many of the benefits of the empathic gift, such as understanding others and being able to heal them, but you are plagued by struggle, as well. Bogged down like this, you cannot function and need to learn to overcome the struggles in order to survive and thrive as an empath.

60-79: You have the empathic gift and it is strong. You need to be careful of overextending yourself with this gift. You have many of the benefits, but many of the issues that plague the empath threaten you. The rest of this book will address how to overcome these struggles and become the best empath you can be.

80-100: You have an incredible amount of empathy. Your empathic gift is stronger than most other empaths, but so are the issues and struggles that come along with gift. You must mind your habits and lifestyle choices carefully if you are to survive this strong of a gift. The rest of this book will help you on your way.

4 Understanding Your Empathic Nature

THERE ARE TWO SIDES TO the empathic gift that you possess. There is the positive, healing side of the gift and the negative, draining side of the gift. First, we will investigate the positive potential that this gift has and then, the struggles and dangers of it.

Positive Potential

The empathic gift has the potential to be one of the most important assets humankind possesses: it can heal emotional wounds opened by tragedy, war, crime, and abuse.

There have always been diseases and conditions that even the most modern human medicine cannot cure. These diseases include such things as emotional problems as well as the sadness of losing a loved one to cancer, the horror of seeing one's home blown apart in war, the terror of having been a victim of rape, or the lingering trauma of having been abused as a child.

Empaths can relate to sufferers on a level that most people cannot. While empaths might not have experienced war, famine, crime, abuse, or any other tragedy themselves, they can feel on a very deep and real level what it means to have experienced such things. Often, just having someone care and truly relate is what helps victims of these experiences heal.

Obviously, these experiences are the extremes of the tragedy and brokenness that plagues our world, but even in less extreme cases, such as a breakup, a fight between friends, the illness of a child, or the loss of a job, empaths are able to relate and help carry the burden of these things. The healing nature of the empath—the willingness to bear the burden of certain experiences and their emotional fallout—helps the world become a kinder place.

In addition, the empath has an incredible capacity for creativity and expression. Many times, your empathic gift will allow you to communicate what others cannot. A victim of war might have no idea how to express what the war was like, but in talking to the person, you come to have some idea and are able to write a poem, draw a picture, or express in some way what that experience was like. Empaths are like a bridge between those who are hurting and the rest of society. An empath takes the hurt that individuals are feeling and communicates it to the members of society chosen by the individual in a way that they can understand.

In other words, empaths are the key to a better society. They are the key to becoming more compassionate toward those who are broken-hearted for one reason or another. If you are an empath, your gift comes with a responsibility—a destiny, even—to change the world for the better.

At the same time, you must be aware of the struggles and dangers that you face as an empath. Let us look at these difficulties and discover how to steer clear of them.

Struggles And Dangers

There are three main areas in which empaths struggle: mental health, addictions, and relationships. We will take a look at each of these types of struggles in order to gain a better understanding of how your empathic gift can function (or malfunction).

Mental Health Issues

First, your empathic gift can be so overwhelming that your mental health suffers. You might even be diagnosed with bipolar disorder, borderline personality disorder, attention deficit disorder, generalized anxiety disorder, social anxiety, or agoraphobia. Although you may not actually have one of these disorders, it is not unusual for an empath to struggle with the same symptoms.

Wild mood swings are a telltale sign that you are an empath, but they can be mistaken for bipolar or borderline personality disorder. Depression is a common side effect of being an empath, since you absorb the emotions and energy around you and so much of the world's energy is negative.

It is also easy to be mistakenly diagnosed with attention deficit disorder, since your surroundings are so filled with stimuli that your mind cannot choose where to focus your attention. Your brain must process so many things are once, as you are not only processing your own reality but the realities of anyone around you, that you will seem disengaged with the outside world.

Anxiety is another common diagnosis for empaths. This diagnosis is prevalent because empaths are often very anxious about the negative energies they are receiving. You might become anxious in a crowd, for example, because you are overstimulated. You are receiving so much energy that it is unclear to your brain how you should handle it. This will make you anxious in that moment and memory will trigger a stress response the next time that you face a crowd. This can manifest as general anxiety, or more specifically as social anxiety, where interacting with others and absorbing their emotions causes you anxiety.

Finally, some empaths are diagnosed with agoraphobia. Agoraphobia is the fear of crowds and manifests often as the fear of leaving one's house. Many empaths have this fear, but it is not entirely unfounded. Leaving your home means interacting with people who likely have negative energy and who will likely steal your positive energy. Therefore, being afraid of leaving your house makes sense and is not just an issue of anxiety. However, agoraphobia is still debilitating to you as a person, hindering your participation in the normal functions of life.

Addictions

Addictions and bad habits are a common problem for empaths. You do not need to be ashamed if you have an addiction; this is simply your method of coping with an overload of emotions. Addictions may give you a sense of control that you do not have in your emotional life and seem to help in the short-term, but they will obviously cost you in the long run. Luckily, there are ways to overcome these addictions or more minor bad habits, which we will cover briefly in this section. However, this is just a brief overview of some common addictions, and should not be taken as medical advice. If you think you struggle with any addiction or mental health problem, you should consult a trained professional and licensed medical doctor.

First, you might have an eating disorder, whether it be eating too much (binge-eating), eating too little (anorexia), or purging (bulimia). These kinds of addictive behaviors definitely fall in the category of giving you a sense of control. They can be very dangerous, and most often require professional help from doctors and therapists in order to break the cycle.

You might be addicted to some sort of substance, whether it be an illicit or prescription drug or alcohol. This often is a form of escapism— a way to avoid feeling the emotions and negative energies that have filtered into your mind, heart, and spirit. These are also very dangerous, and a professional will often need to intervene to provide you with accountability and support.

For mild unhealthy habits, like eating too much junk food, or having a few glasses of wine each night, you can try to replace these habits with newer healthier ones. Things to remember in trying to break these negative habits: First, always replace a negative with a positive. Whenever you are cutting out a behavior or substance, you need to replace it with a positive habit or activity that you enjoy and that satisfies your craving. Second, you need to interrupt the pattern. If you know that whenever you are finished with work and you go home, your tendency is to drink alcohol, then change up your routine and go to the gym after work or go out with a friend. Third, try not to tempt yourself by having the substance to which you are prone to overuse close at hand, or try making the activity less accessible. This might mean not buying alcohol or junk food.

Whatever choices you make in trying to break your addictions or negative habits, remember that ending your negative habits depends on the maintenance of your mental, emotional, and spiritual health. If you do not remain healthy in your mind, heart, and spirit, then your addiction could return any time you have a tough moment. This means that at the same time as you are working on breaking the addiction that you have, you need to improve your empathic abilities and skills to care for yourself in such a way as to become self-supporting and self-encouraging.

Relationships

Empaths often experience relationship problems and even enter toxic relationships. There are three types of toxic relationships into which empaths often fall: codependent relationships, abusive relationships, and parasitic relationships. Sometimes these relationship models overlap, so one relationship can fall into more than one category. Each one is dangerous in its own way and must be handled differently when trying to extract yourself.

The first type of relationship mentioned, the codependent relationship, is one in which you, the empath, define yourself by how you relate to another person so that outside that person's existence, you do not know who you are. You might be "Levi's mom" or "Nancy's husband" or "Richard's friend," but no matter by whom you define yourself, you do not know that you could go on without them. This goes beyond the normal fear of losing a loved one: you are absolutely terrified that, without them, you would have nothing.

The second type of relationship is the abusive relationship. In this type of relationship, the other person abuses you, the empath, using your willingness to take the blame for mistreatment. The abuser takes advantage of the abused in a physical, emotional, or sexual way, and the abused feels shame and guilt as though he or she is responsible for the abuse.

The last type of relationship is the parasitic relationship. This is a one-way relationship in which the parasitic individual takes advantage of the empath's listening ear and generous heart to get the empath to carry his or her burdens. Instead of asking the empath to share his or her emotional load, the individual shoves the entire burden onto the empath. The parasitic person never asks about the empath and never shows concern for him or her. Instead, in this type of relationship, the concern goes only one way. This puts the strain in the relationship on you, the empath.

We will discuss how to recognize these relationships and how to gracefully avoid or exit them in the next chapter.

5 PROTECTING YOUR ENERGY

THE MOST DANGEROUS THING IN the world to empaths is toxic people. Toxic people and toxic relationships drain empaths of their positive energy without offering anything but negative energy in return. To avoid or escape toxic relationships, you first need to learn to recognize them.

In this chapter, we will discover the traits of the various types of toxic relationships: the codependent relationship, the abusive relationship, and the parasitic relationship. Then, we will look at how to carefully and kindly remove yourself from such relationships and discover some tips for avoiding such relationships in the future.

Codependent Relationships

As mentioned in the last chapter, the codependent relationship is a relationship in which you define yourself by your relationship to the other person. You might be spouse, mother, sister, brother, father, son, or friend. Whatever you are, you see that as your primary identity, and should that person for some reason leave or pass on, you feel you would have nothing and no identity.

Again, this goes beyond the normal amount of grief one would feel at the loss of the other person. Instead, you feel hopeless at the thought of losing this person.

This type of relationship is marked by a few signs, which are as follows. First, you feel at ease only around this other person, and if he or she leaves the area where you are, you begin to feel incredibly uncomfortable. Second, you feel happiest in life when you are helping this other person, so much so that you prefer to be helping him or her than doing anything else in the world, even taking care of yourself. Third, you would do anything for this person, especially if threatened with him or her leaving the relationship.

As you might have guessed, this is a toxic relationship because it gives you no time or energy for caring for yourself. You are constantly thinking about the other person in the friendship or relationship. You forego self-care for this person's sake and, as a result, you begin to wither. This makes you desperate for purpose, which you take to mean you need to invest more in this relationship, which drains you more. It is an endless and vicious cycle.

Abusive Relationships

Abusive relationships can manifest in various ways: emotional, physical, verbal, sexual, neglectful, etc. These types of relationships are characterized by the putting down of one of the individuals in the relationship, likely the empath. This can be done through calling the empath names, forcing sexual intimacy with the empath, hitting or kicking the empath, or by implying lack of worth in the empath.

The emotionally abusive relationship is the type of abusive relationship that is the hardest to define but also is the one in which most empaths find themselves. In many ways, this is a relationship of manipulation. It might be as overt as the other person saying something like, "If you can't _____ for me then you are nothing to me!" or it might be as sly as the other person asking, "Don't you love me? Why won't you _____ then?"

Abusive relationships confuse the empath, especially with their general sense of responsibility whenever something goes wrong in a relationship. You might begin to doubt your self-worth because of emotional or verbal abuse, or you will berate yourself for not wanting to be intimate with your partner in cases of sexual abuse. You may think, "Surely, he or she is just expressing love for me, and I cannot accept it," right? This is not the case, I assure you.

Your worth is not wrapped up in what the other person communicates or thinks about you. You are far worthier of affection than the manipulating standards that have been set by your partner. You are far more precious than the measure of your acts of kindness toward your best friend. You are far more capable of love than just the care you can show in one relationship. You are an empath: you feel deeply and express emotion in ways that many people could not hope to do in their entire lives.

If you are in an abusive relationship, it is important to get help from trusted friends or family, or even law enforcement.

Parasitic Relationships

Parasitic relationships are another form of toxic relationship. Remember, first of all, that being in a parasitic relationship and being in an abusive relationship or a codependent relationship are not mutually exclusive. The parasitic relationship, however, has different signs for which you can watch.

First, parasitic people never ask about your well-being nor do they show any signs of interest in your life. Your conversations are always about their lives and concerns, and should the conversation turn to your life, they will quickly interject how something from their own lives relates and use that as a platform to continue speaking about themselves. You know instinctively never to call these people when you need help or someone to listen to your struggles.

Second, in parasitic relationships, you always feel drained. You, the empath, feel like the other person is sucking the energy and life out of you, which, in fact, is the case. The parasitic person exchanges his or her negative energy for your positive energy and thereby replaces any spiritual positivity you might have had with despondency, fear, anxiety, depression, and despair.

Third, the parasitic person often does not have any other friends, or if he or she does, the other friends are also empaths. This is because most parasitic people latch onto those of whom they can take advantage. Other than empaths, most people will not put up with the one-way nature of the relationship with these parasitic individuals for long. Thus, if you are someone's only or best friend despite the fact that he or she knows next to nothing about you, you can be sure that you are in a parasitic relationship.

Avoiding and Exiting Toxic Relationships

Most empaths, as you might suspect, can spot a parasitic, abusive, or codependent person a mile away. The reason they become blinded is because they are caught up in problem-solving and the desire to heal and do not remember to guard themselves and protect their energy.

The first line of protection when facing a potential codependent, abuser, or parasite is to take a moment to evaluate the spiritual energy that you are receiving from this person. Is the energy of a codependent, abusive, or parasitic personality? Are they overly needy, jealous, possessive, or manipulative? If so, take a moment to decide to hold back. Use the few seconds before entering a conversation with them to decide whether to withhold your full energy from the interaction. Refrain from engaging at all if possible, but if not, keep the conversation at the level of small talk, and do not offer more of your energy than is necessary.

A second line of defense is to keep your life filled with positive people. That is, fill your time and your schedule with positive relationships and kind people so that you will literally have no time for the codependents, abusers, and parasites that seek to eat up your energy and your life. Empaths have a very difficult time lying or misrepresenting the truth, so you will need a legitimate excuse if you want to get out of a potential commitment to a toxic relationship. What better way to excuse yourself than to fill your life with good energy and positivity?

One thing you need to keep at the forefront of your mind in these toxic interactions is that "helping" these people actually hurts them. It allows them to unload without consequences to themselves. Codependents will never develop a true sense of self, and should you ever need to leave for some reason or another without warning, you would leave the codependent feeling debilitated and disabled. Ignoring the warning signs of an abusive person reinforces his or her idea that his worth far outweighs your own and allows him or her to carry those ideas to the rest of his or her interactions. Allowing a parasitic person to use you tells him or her that other people do not matter, keeping them from the type of intimacy that we all desire deep-down because they cannot recognize the two-way flow of a good relationship. You must realize that your "helping" these types of people is truly only hurting them, and this will help remove the blinders that your desire to heal puts on you. Healing comes through tough love sometimes, and you need to know when that is the case.

Of course, even the most vigilant empath may fall into a toxic relationship. It is important to remember that it is not your fault. In the case that you need to leave a toxic relationship, however, the best option is gracious honesty. To the parasite, you might say something like, "I feel like this relationship is very one-sided." To the abuser you might tell, "I love you, but your actions and words hurt me, so I need some space to rebuild myself." To the codependent, you might say, "It seems like we have gotten our identities all mixed up together, and I think it would be good for both of us to find our own selves for a little while." Being honest while maintaining a sense of kindness and respect will keep you from feeling the guilt you would if you gave a reason that was false or misconstrued. Honesty is the only way to truly free yourself from these relationships.

6 THRIVING WITH YOUR GIFT

NOW THAT WE HAVE COVERED the drawbacks to being an empath, you might be wondering if it is even possible to thrive when you have the empathic gift. It is! There are certain guidelines and tips you must use, but when an empath finds his or her rhythm, happiness isn't a strong enough word to describe the feeling. You feel more deeply than most people, meaning that, yes, you feel deeper levels of pain, but you also reach higher heights of joy and hope. How can you reach these heights? Let's look at some ways to ensure your success and happiness as an empath.

Respecting Your Limitations

The first thing that you must remember when you are seeking to thrive as an empath is to work within your limitations. The very fact that you have limitations may make you feel confined, like you are in a cage and can't break free. You want to defy the limitations, not work within them. However, you must remember that the things outside your limitations are what actually enslave you: negativity, toxic relationships, and draining situations.

For example, you need to avoid crowds and charged situations as much as possible. If you know there will be a rally downtown tomorrow, try to do your shopping there today. This is not really meant to limit you but to set you free to do what you really want to do in life: find happiness and give healing to those around you. The negative emotions of anger and frustration could entrap you and drain your energy if you are not careful.

Another thing you might want to limit or avoid is your consumption of media. The news, Facebook, Twitter, Instagram, and other forms of media all drain you without offering anything in return. If you want to have energy for your friends and family — those you truly love — try to limit your consumption of media. Giving away your energy to the boy on TV who just lost his mother does not heal him and drains you. Saving your energy to comfort your friend who just broke up with her long-term boyfriend will make a positive impact in her life and in turn will help you feel fulfilled.

Creating Positive Relationships

What does a positive relationship look like? How does it function, and how do you go about developing one?

First, a positive relationship is two-sided. Concern and loving affection flow both ways in the relationship. You and your best friend each ask about the other's well-being, are there for each other when things go wrong in life, rejoice when the other person has a stroke of good fortune, and carry each other's burdens as though they were your own, sharing the load of care.

Second, in positive relationships, the two individuals are interdependent. This means that they rely on each other as well as think about how their decisions will affect the other person. They are not simply dependent, wanting the other person to do all the work for them, but nor are they independent, not caring how the other person feels. In a positive, interdependent relationship, your boyfriend or girlfriend will think about you in his or her financial, social, emotional, career, etc. decisions because he or she knows that such decisions impact you as well.

How does one develop such a beautiful relationship or friendship? There are a few ways these types of relationships can develop. First, you need to share life together. Do activities together, whether it be outdoor activities like hiking, boating, rafting, hunting, or fishing, or indoor activities like taking a cooking class, learning to dance, going out for a meal, or practicing a hobby together. A relationship includes talking, but it is about shared experience as much as it is about understanding what each person has experienced and is experiencing. Share your friends and family, as well. This will communicate trust and investment in the relationship when you share the new person with the people closest to you. Share both surface and deep thoughts. Do not limit yourself to one or the other, but allow the conversation to take you where it will.

Additionally, remember not to take things too fast or to try to force things with someone. Your tendency as an empath is to rush headlong into incredible depth, but as you will recall from this book and from experience, this will leave you in an uncomfortable place of intimacy before you are ready for it. This is another reason that sharing your life is a good idea. It will give you some shared experiences to discuss so that you do not have to spill your entire life story in the first meeting. With a new friend or a potential partner, keeping things more surface-level at first is generally a good idea until you can properly gauge whether you want to invest.

Another way to develop good relationships is to find creative ways to express your affection for the other person and encourage him or her to do the same. You might be used to getting jewelry for your girlfriend for Christmas and her birthday, and while jewelry might be well-received, try to add a creative love poem or something you made to the gift to show her you really appreciate her. Creative ways of expressing your affection feeds your care for the other person and will increase his or her investment in the relationship as well. It also allows you to thrive as an empath by requiring you to use your gift of artistic creativity and imagination.

Discovering Happiness

First, spend as much time in nature as you can, but at least as much as you need to maintain your positive energy. Do not apologize for needing this time to yourself. Without your store of positive energy, you are giving away borrowed energy that will turn into negative energy the next time you have a chance to breathe and relax for a moment. Giving away borrowed energy takes a great toll on you, and you will need to then spend time communing with nature for even longer to replenish your supply. If you maintain a good balance of time spent with people and time spent alone in nature, you will never be depleted entirely, and you will feel an underlying happiness and stability despite all of life's storms.

Participate in art therapy as well. This will unleash your creative spirit and help you to express and thereby release the energy of your interactions throughout the day. Being creative releases the negative energies from your spirit, mind, and heart. This is important for your sense of happiness, because negative energy depletes your happiness, while positive energy increases it. By getting rid of negative energy, you make room for positive energy, which therefore increases your sense of joy.

Journaling is another good practice to take up. Journaling helps release and process the negative energies and things that happen through the day. Journaling regularly can help you as an empath understand what is causing you difficulty and pain and thereby help you to release those pieces of negativity without letting go of what is positive.

Faith practices and spiritual practices can also be vital to finding, maintaining, and growing one's happiness as an empath. Faith practices include yoga, prayer, meditation, reading scriptures, attending religious services, and discussing spiritual topics with others of the faith. These things help give a structure around which an empath can organize his or her life without feeling trapped, if organized wisely. This also gives a paradigm through which to see and understand the world. Faith practices give another way to see events in one's life as part of a grander picture and help the empath remember how his or her destiny fits into the larger scheme of things. Faith practices also relax the mind so that negative energies can be released, whether back into the spirit of the world or to a deity in prayer.

With these practices and principles, as well as with those you discover yourself along the way, you will no doubt be successful in attaining happiness and thriving as an empath.

7 Conclusion

Now that you have finished this book, I hope you are encouraged in your journey as an empath. It is not an easy path, but it is a life-changing one. You have now learned how to tell if you are an empath and how to test others for the empathic gift. In the process, you learned about twenty characteristics of the empath, including character traits, relationship behavior, lifestyle, others' reactions, and struggles.

We looked at the struggles more closely in Chapter Three. I hope you are not discouraged, but rather find this to be a worthy challenge. You are blessed with the empathic gift because you have a destiny to help make this world a better, more compassionate place. Your responsibility is to yourself to be the best you can be. Knowing that these struggles exist for you means that you need to steer clear of them as best you can, and you need to seek help when you do fall victim to them. Addictions are especially nasty beasts because of the stigma that society places on them, but you must know that the cost of keeping them up is much higher than the price of getting help. Your life could be forfeit in an overdose or in jail, so take heart and get professional help if you are struggling with any of these addiction issues.

Relationship problems are another type of issue. Between codependent, abusive, and parasitic relationships, the empath has a lot of room to fall into toxic relationships with other people. However, as many people as there are that are codependent, abusive, or parasitic, there are so many more empaths or kind-hearted people who are willing to befriend you. It might take some effort to find them and develop a relationship, but you will be more than satisfied once you have that positive person in your life.

As I encouraged you before, there are many ways for the empath to live, survive, and even thrive with the empathic gift. Empathy is not a curse, but a blessing whether you believe it is from a god or from the World Spirit or just an innate ability. Empathy is what brings the world closer together in harmony and peace, in understanding and desire to live together with unity. You are the bridge between the hurting of the world, which is most of us, and those who would like to help, which is many of us, as well. Without you, the helpers would have a hard time understanding the needs of the hurting. Using your gift, you can be a translator, through art and speech, telling the world how to heal its wounds and how to bring harmony to the brokenness that we see. So, with that, I would like to say thank you. Thank you for picking up this book and being willing to use your empathic gift for the good of those around you. The world will be eternally grateful.

Your Feedback is Important to Me

Dear Reader,

Thank you for taking the time to read this book. I hope you got a lot out of it and learned something you can apply to your own life.

If you have any feedback, positive or negative, I'd love to hear from you. I personally read all the reviews on my Amazon page, and hope you'll take a minute to tell me (and other readers) what you think.

Type this URL into your browser to go straight to the review page for this book: bit.ly/empathreview

Thank you!

—Rozella Hart

Made in the USA
Monee, IL
11 May 2020